Ju'

by Ei

Illustrated by Robert Bartelt

Julius was a penguin. Eddie, the keeper at the zoo, always called him Percy but Julius never paid any attention. After all, he was an Emperor penguin, and he needed the name of an Emperor.

Julius was a very lonely Emperor penguin. All the other penguins had families. Every afternoon they lined up together for the Penguin Parade, but not Julius.

Then one fine winter afternoon, Julius found the egg. It didn't really look like the eggs that the other penguins had, but it was the best he could do.

Julius rolled the egg on to his feet and kept it warm with his soft feathery tummy.

"I shall hatch the egg," thought Julius, happily, "and I shall have a chick of my very own."

Julius had often watched the other father penguins standing patiently and proudly, hatching the eggs. How he had wished that he could join them.

6

Eddie, the keeper, watched
Julius and sighed.

"Come on, Percy, old lad," he
said, kindly. "That egg will never
hatch."

You see, Julius had not found
an egg. He had found a hard old
bun that a visitor had thrown to
the penguins.

"Get off, Percy, old lad," said
Eddie again.

Perhaps if Eddie had called Julius by his proper name, he would have listened. Instead he took no notice and stayed on his bun for day after day.

He had nothing to eat and nothing to drink. Emperor penguins stay on their eggs for two whole months. They don't think about food or water. They think about the little chick that is going to hatch.

"That bun will crumble away," thought Eddie, "and poor old Percy will starve to death waiting for it to hatch. I must do something."

He told his wife, Nancy, about his problem.

"That's easy," said Nancy. "Get him another egg."

"There aren't any," said Eddie, sadly.

"It doesn't have to be a penguin's egg, does it?" said Nancy.

"You're a wonder, Nancy," said Eddie. He gave Nancy a great big hug and went to see his friend who was a farmer.

The next day, Julius was having
a little doze in the sunshine. Eddie
crept up very quietly. Carefully,
he lifted up Julius's soft feathers.

He took out the crumbly old
bun and he left a real egg there
in its place.

"There you go, Percy, old lad,"
he said.

Julius was very tired and very, very hungry. He opened one eye. He might have opened both eyes if Eddie had called him by his proper name.

He looked down at his feet. His egg felt strange: hard and warm.

"It's going to hatch soon," thought Julius. "That's it. That's why it's different."

He was too happy and excited
to go back to sleep.

"It's hatching," he told all the
other penguins, as they lined up
for the parade.

"It will be tomorrow at the latest," he told his friends as they set off to teach their new chicks to swim. "We'll join you soon."

Next morning, Julius felt
something move. He lifted his
tummy and there lay a broken
egg shell.

A strange little chick lay on the shell and it blinked several times at Julius. Then the baby rolled off Julius's feet.

Julius watched as the baby
picked himself up, shook out his
feathers and then ran straight
back to the comfort of Julius's soft
warm tummy.

"Hello, Daddy," he said.

"Daddy. I am a daddy," thought Julius. "I have never been so happy!"

"Welcome, young man," he
said to the chick. "Do you know
that you are an Emperor
Penguin? I shall call you Augustus.
That is an Emperor's name."

Augustus peeped out from under Julius's tummy. He could see lots of grass. He could see a lovely big pond.

"Come along, Augustus," said Julius. "It's time to meet our friends."

He waddled off to the pond
followed by his little yellow baby.

"Such a fine baby," Julius
proudly told the other penguins.

The other penguins looked
very hard at baby Augustus.

"He's a very strange penguin,
Julius," they said, "but he looks
like a nice lad. He'll make a fine
swimmer ... with those lovely
wide webbed feet."

And, of course, the new baby
was a wonderful swimmer, almost
as good as his father. Eddie had
been very clever. Augustus, or
Donald, as Eddie always called
him, was a duck.